9/4/19

ROBERT LOUIS STEVENSON

Robert Louis Stevenson

WITH NUMEROUS ILLUSTRATIONS

FOLCROFT LIBRARY EDITIONS / 1972

Library of Congress Cataloging in Publication Data
Main entry under title:

Robert Louis Stevenson.

    CONTENTS: Nicoll, W. R. The personality and style
of Robert Louis Stevenson.--Chesterton, G. K. The
characteristics of Robert Louis Stevenson.--Nicoll,
W. R. Home from the hill. [etc.]
    1. Stevenson, Robert Louis, 1850-1894.
I. Stevenson, Robert Louis, 1850-1894. II. Nicoll,
Sir William Robertson, 1851-1923. III. Chesterton,
Gilbert Keith, 1874-
PR5493.R6 1972   828'.8'09   72-13050
ISBN 0-8414-1140-9 (lib. bdg.)

Limited 100 Copies

Manufactured in the United States of America

Folcroft Library Editions
Box 182
Folcroft, Pa. 19032

Robert Louis Stevenson

WITH NUMEROUS ILLUSTRATIONS

London

HODDER AND STOUGHTON

27, Paternoster Row

1902

PRINTED BY
HAZELL, WATSON AND VINEY, LD,
LONDON AND AYLESBURY.

LIST OF ILLUSTRATIONS

THE PERSONALITY AND STYLE OF
ROBERT LOUIS STEVENSON

AS the years pass they disengage the virtue of a writer, and decide whether or not he has force enough to live. Will Stevenson live? Undoubtedly. He is far more secure of immortality than many very popular writers. The sale of his books may not be great, and he may even disappear from the marts of literature now and then, but he will always be revived, and it may turn out that his reputation may wear as well as that of Charles Lamb. For he engages his readers by the double gift of personality and style.

The personality of Stevenson is strangely arresting. In the first place it was a double personality. In his journey to the Cevennes he reflects that every one of us travels about with a donkey. In his "Strange Case of Dr. Jekyll and Mr. Hyde," the donkey becomes a devil. Every Jekyll is haunted by his Hyde. Somebody said that "The Strange Case of Dr. Jekyll and Mr. Hyde" showed Stevenson as Poe, with the addition of a moral sense. Critics may differ as to the exact literary value of the famous little book, but as an expression of Stevenson's deepest thought about life it will retain its interest. He was not content to dwell in a world where the lines are drawn clear, where the sheep are separated from the goats. He would have a foot in both worlds, content to dwell neither wholly with the sheep nor wholly with the goats. No doubt his ruling interest was in ethical problems, and he could be stern in

1

his moral judgments, as, for example, in his discussion of the character of Burns. He was by nature and training religious, " something of the Shorter Catechist." His earliest publication was a defence of the Covenanters, and in his last days he established close friendships with the Samoan missionaries. Yet he was by no means " orthodox," either in ethics or in religion. Much as he wrote on conduct, there were certain subjects, and these the most difficult, on which he never spoke out. On love, for example, and all that goes with it, it

From a photo kindly supplied by Mr. Graham Balfour

THE REV. LEWIS BALFOUR IN HIS YOUTH

is quite certain that he never spoke his full mind to the public at least.

Another very striking quality in his personality was his fortitude. He was simply the bravest of men. Now and then, as in his letter to George Meredith, he lets us see under what disabling conditions he fought his battle. Human beings in a world like this are naturally drawn to one who suffers, and will not let himself be mastered or corrupted by suffering. They do not care for the prosperous, dominant, athletic, rich and long-lived man. They may conjecture, indeed, that behind all the bravery there is much hidden pain, but if it is not revealed to them they cannot be sure.

From a photo kindly supplied by Mr. Graham Balfour

THE REV. LEWIS BALFOUR, GRANDFATHER OF ROBERT LOUIS STEVENSON

NO. 8, HOWARD PLACE,
EDINBURGH

The House where
Robert Louis Stevenson was born
on the 13th November, 1850

*From a photo by
J. Patrick, Edinburgh*

They love Charles Lamb for the manner in which he went through his trial, and they love him none the less because he was sometimes overborne, because on occasions he stumbled and fell. Charlotte Brontë was an example of fortitude as remarkable as Stevenson, but she was not brave after the same manner. She allowed the clouds to thicken over her life and make it grey. Stevenson sometimes found himself in the dust, but he recovered and rose up to speak fresh words of cheer. He took thankfully and eagerly whatever life had to offer him in the way of affection, of kindness, of admiration. Nor did he ever in any trouble lose his belief that the Heart of things was kind. In the face of all obstacle he went steadily on with his work, nor did he ever allow himself to fall below the best that he could do. An example so touching, so rare, so admirable, is a

THOMAS STEVENSON, FATHER OF ROBERT LOUIS STEVENSON

From a photo by J. Patrick, Edinburgh
NO. 17, HERIOT ROW, EDINBURGH
In May, 1857, Robert Louis Stevenson's parents took up their abode at 17, Heriot Row, which remained the family headquarters until the death of Thomas Stevenson, in 1887

reinforcement which weary humanity cannot spare.

With these qualities, and, indeed, as their natural result, Stevenson had a rare courtesy. He was, in the words of the old Hebrew song, "lovely and pleasant," or rather, as Robertson Smith translated it, "lovely and winsome," in all his bearings to men of all kinds, so long as they did not fall under the condemnation of his moral judgment. With a personality so rich, Stevenson had the power of communicating himself. He could reveal his personality without egotism, without offence. Many writers of charming

ROBERT LOUIS STEVENSON
AT THE AGE OF SIX

COLINTON MANSE

The Residence of
Stevenson's Maternal
Grandfather

*From a photo by
J. Patrick, Edinburgh*

individuality cannot show themselves in their books.   There is as little
of themselves in their novels as there would be in a treatise on
mathematics, if they could write it.   Perhaps less.   There have been
mathematicians like Augustus de Morgan, who could put humour
and personality into a book on geometry.

But Stevenson had not only a personality, he had a style.   His
golden gift of words can never be denied.   He may sometimes have
been too " precious," but the power of writing as he could write is so
uncommon that he must always stand with a very few.   We believe
that Stevenson's style is largely an expression of his courtesy.   He
wished as a matter of mere politeness and goodwill to express himself
as well as he could.   In fact, it was this courtesy that led him to his
famous paradox about the end of art, his characterisation of the artist
as the Son of Joy.   "The French have a romantic evasion for one

employment, and call its practitioners the Daughters of Joy. The artist is of the same family : he is of the Sons of Joy, chooses his trade to please himself, gains his livelihood by pleasing others, and has parted with something of the sterner dignity of man." The theory that all art is decoration cannot be seriously considered. It was certainly not true of Stevenson's art. He wished to please, but he had other and higher ends. He had to satisfy his exacting conscience, and he obeyed its demands sincerely and righteously, and to the utmost of his power. But he was too good a man to be satisfied even with that. Milton put into all his work the most passionate labour, but he did not believe that pleasure was the end of art. Nor would he have been satisfied by complying with his conscience. He had a message to deliver, and he delivered it in the most effective forms at his command. Stevenson had his message, too, and uttered it right memorably. If

MRS. THOMAS STEVENSON, MOTHER OF ROBERT LOUIS STEVENSON

the message had to be put in a few words, they would be these : *Good my soul, be brave!*   He was bold enough to call Tennyson a **Son of Joy**, but he would have assented with all his soul to Tennyson's lines:

> And here the singer for his art
> Not all in vain may plead :
> The song that nerves the nation's heart
> Is in itself a deed.

W. ROBERTSON NICOLL.

THE CHARACTERISTICS OF
ROBERT LOUIS STEVENSON

ALL things and all men are underrated, much by others, especially by themselves: and men grow tired of men just as they do of green grass, so that they have to seek for green carnations. All great men possess in themselves the qualities which will certainly lay them open to censure and diminishment; but these inevitable deficiencies in the greatness of great men vary in the widest degree of variety.

From a photo kindly supplied by
Dr. H. Bellyse Baildon
MR. THOMAS STEVENSON AND HIS
SON, WHEN LOUIS WAS TEN YEARS OLD

From a photo kindly supplied by
Dr. H. Bellyse Baildon
A PHOTOGRAPH OF ROBERT LOUIS
STEVENSON IN FANCY DRESS

ROBERT LOUIS STEVENSON AT THE
AGE OF 15

Stevenson is open to a particularly subtle, a particularly effective and a particularly unjust disparagement. The advantage of great men like Blake or Browning or Walt Whitman is that they did not observe the niceties of technical literature. The far greater disadvantage of Stevenson is that he did. Because he had a conscience about small matters in art, he is conceived not to have had an imagination about big ones. It is assumed by some that he must have been a bad architect, and the only reason that they can assign is that he was a good workman. The mistake which has given rise to this conception is one that has much to answer for in numerous departments of modern art, literature, religion, philosophy, and politics. The supreme and splendid characteristic of Stevenson, was his levity; and his levity was the flower of a hundred grave philosophies. The strong man is always light: the weak man is always heavy. A swift and casual agility is the mark of bodily strength: a humane levity is the mark of spiritual strength. A thoroughly strong man swinging a sledge-hammer can tap the top of an eggshell. A

ROBERT LOUIS STEVENSON
AT THE AGE OF 20

ALISON
CUNNINGHAM
("CUMMY")

weaker man swinging a sledge-hammer will break the table on which it stands into pieces. Also, if he is a very weak man, he will be proud of having broken the table, and call himself a strong man dowered with the destructive power of an Imperial race.

This is, superficially speaking, the peculiar interest of Stevenson. He had what may be called a perfect mental athleticism, which enabled him to leap from crag to crag, and to trust himself anywhere and upon any question. His splendid quality as an essayist and controversialist was that he could always recover his weapon. He was not like the average swashbuckler of the current parties, tugged at the tail of his own sword. This is what tends, for example, to make him stand out so well beside his unhappy friend Mr. Henley, whose true and un-questionable affection has lately taken so bitter and feminine a form.

From a drawing by A. S. Boyd
ROBERT LOUIS STEVENSON
Reproduced from Dr. H. B. Baildon's " Life of Robert Louis Stevenson,"
by kind permission of Messrs. Chatto & Windus

ROBERT LOUIS STEVENSON
AT THE AGE OF 25

Mr. Henley, an admirable poet and critic, is, nevertheless, the man *par excellence* who breaks the table instead of tapping the egg. In his recent article on Stevenson he entirely misses this peculiar and supreme point about his subject.

He there indulged in a very emotional remonstrance against the reverence almost universally paid to the physical misfortunes of his celebrated friend. " If Stevenson was a stricken man," he said, " are we not all stricken men ?" And he proceeded to call up the images of the poor and sick, and of their stoicism under their misfortunes. If sentimentalism be definable as the permitting of an emotional movement to cloud a clear intellectual distinction, this most assuredly is sentimentalism, for it would be impossible more completely to misunderstand the real nature of the cult of the courage of Stevenson. The reason that Stevenson has been selected out of the whole of suffering humanity as the type of this more modern and occult martyrdom is a very simple one. It is not that he merely contrived, like any other man of reasonable manliness, to support pain and limitation without whimpering or committing suicide or taking to drink. In that sense of course we are all stricken men and we are all stoics. The ground of Stevenson's particular

ROBERT LOUIS STEVENSON IN THE
" BART.'S " HAT, 1876

From a photo kindly supplied by Mr. Graham Balfour
CHALET LA SOLITUDE, HYÈRES
Where Robert Louis Stevenson lived from March, 1883,
to July, 1884

fascination in this matter was that he was the exponent, and the successful exponent, not merely of negative manliness, but of a positive and lyric gaiety. This wounded soldier did not merely refrain from groans, he gave forth instead a war song, so juvenile and inspiriting that thousands of men without a scratch went back into the battle. This cripple did not merely bear his own burdens, but those of thousands of contemporary men. No one can feel anything but the most inexpressible kind of reverence for the patience of the asthmatic charwoman or the consumptive tailor's assistant. Still the charwoman does not write "Aes Triplex," nor the tailor "The Child's Garden of Verses." Their stoicism is magnificent, but it is stoicism. But Stevenson did not face his troubles as a stoic, he faced them as an Epicurean. He practised with an austere triumph that terrible asceticism of frivolity which is so much more difficult than the asceticism of gloom. His resignation can only be called an active and uproarious resignation. It was not merely self-sufficing, it was infectious. His triumph was, not that he went through his misfortunes without becoming a cynic or a poltroon, but that he went through his misfortunes and emerged quite exceptionally cheerful and reasonable and courteous, quite exceptionally light-hearted and liberal-minded. His triumph was, in other words, that he went through his misfortunes and did not become like Mr. Henley.

There is one aspect of this matter in particular, which it is as well

From a photo by Mendelssohn

MRS. ROBERT LOUIS STEVENSON

The marriage of Mr. and Mrs. Robert Louis Stevenson took place in San Francisco in the Spring of 1880

Mrs Robert Louis Stevenson

A
PHOTOGRAPH
TAKEN DURING
ROBERT LOUIS
STEVENSON'S
SECOND VISIT TO
AMERICA
IN 1887

Lloyd Osbourne   Sport   Robert Louis Stevenson

to put somewhat more clearly before ourselves. This triumph of
Stevenson's over his physical disadvantages is commonly spoken of
with reference only to the elements of joy and faith, and what may
be called the new and essential virtue of cosmic courage. But as a

MOLOKAI, HAWAIIAN ISLANDS, THE TERRIBLE LEPER SETTLEMENT

Which Stevenson visited in May, 1889

From a photo kindly supplied by Mr. Graham Balfour

ROBERT LOUIS STEVENSON AT THE AGE OF 44
From a painting in the National Portrait Gallery, by Percy F. S. Spence

matter of fact the peculiarly interesting detachment of Stevenson from his own body, is exhibited in a quite equally striking way in its purely intellectual aspect. Apart from any moral qualities, Stevenson was characterised by a certain airy wisdom, a certain light and cool rationality, which is very rare and very difficult indeed to those who are greatly thwarted or tormented in life. It is possible to find an invalid capable of the work of a strong man, but it is very rare to find an invalid capable of the idleness of a strong man. It is possible to find an invalid who has the faith which removes mountains,

2

STEVENSON'S HOUSE AT VAILIMA

but not easy to find an invalid who has the faith that puts up with pessimists.   It may not be impossible or even unusual for a man to lie on his back on a sick bed in a dark room and be an optimist. But it is very unusual indeed for a man to lie on his back on a sick bed in a dark room and be a reasonable optimist: and that is what Stevenson, almost alone of modern optimists, succeeded in being.

The faith of Stevenson, like that of a great number of very sane men, was founded on what is called a paradox—the paradox that existence was splendid because it was, to all outward appearance, desperate.   Paradox, so far from being a modern and fanciful matter, is inherent in all the great hypotheses of humanity.   The Athanasian Creed, for example, the supreme testimony of Catholic Christianity, sparkles with paradox like a modern society comedy.   Thus, in the same manner, scientific philosophy tells us that finite space is unthinkable and infinite space is unthinkable.   Thus the most influential modern metaphysician, Hegel, declares without hesitation. when the last rag of theology is abandoned, and the last point of philosophy passed. that existence is the same as non-existence.

ROBERT
LOUIS
STEVENSON

*From
a painting
by
Count Nerli*

Reproduced from
Dr. H. B. Baildon's
" Life of
Robert Louis
Stevenson,"
by kind
permission of
Messrs.
Chatto & Windus

Thus the brilliant author of "Lady Windermere's Fan," in the electric glare of modernity, finds that life is much too important

DINING- AND RECEPTION-HALL IN THE RESIDENCE AT VAILIMA

to be taken seriously. Thus Tertullian, in the first ages of faith, said " Credo quia impossibile."

We must not, therefore, be immediately repelled by this paradoxical character of Stevenson's optimism, or imagine for a moment that it was merely a part of that artistic foppery or " faddling hedonism " with which he has been ridiculously credited. His optimism was one which, so far from dwelling upon those flowers and sunbeams which form the stock-in-trade of conventional optimism, took a peculiar pleasure in the contemplation of skulls, and cudgels, and gallows. It is one thing to be the kind of optimist who can divert his mind from personal suffering by dreaming of the face of an

PORTRAIT OF TUSITALA ("TELLER OF TALES") WITH THE
NATIVE CHIEF TUI-MA-LE-ALII-FANO
Reproduced from " The Vailima Letters " by kind permission of
Messrs. Methuen & Co.

ROBERT LOUIS STEVENSON AND HIS FAVOURITE HORSE "JACK"
(Reproduced from "The Vailima Letters," by kind permission of Messrs. Methuen & Co.)

angel, and quite another thing to be the kind of optimist who can divert it by dreaming of the foul fat face of Long John Silver. And this faith of his had a very definite and a very original philosophical purport. Other men have justified existence because it was a harmony. He justified it because it was a battle, because it was an inspiring and melodious discord. He appealed to a certain set of facts which lie far deeper than any logic—the great paradoxes of the soul. For the singular fact is that the spirit of man is in reality depressed by all the things which, logically speaking, should encourage it, and encouraged by all the things which, logically speaking, should depress it. Nothing, for example, can be conceived more really dispiriting than that rationalistic explanation of pain

MATAAFA, THE "REBEL" KING

Who was defeated and imprisoned in August 1893, upon the
outbreak of war in the Island

which conceives it as a thing laid by Providence upon the worst people. Nothing, on the other hand, can be conceived as more exalting and reassuring than that great mystical doctrine which teaches that pain is a thing laid by Providence upon the best. We can accept the agony of heroes, while we revolt against the agony of culprits. We can all endure to regard pain when it is mysterious; our deepest nature protests against it the moment that it is rational. This doctrine that the best man suffers most is, of course, the supreme doctrine of Christianity: millions have found not merely an elevating but a soothing story in the undeserved sufferings of Christ; had the sufferings been deserved we should all have been pessimists.

Stevenson's great ethical and philo-

TEMBINOKA, THE KING OF APEMAMA

Mrs. Stevenson Mr. Lloyd Mrs. Thomas
Robert Louis Stevenson Osbourne Stevenson

Austin Mr. Graham
Strong Balfour

*From a photo kindly supplied by
Mrs Graham Balfour*

KAVA DRINKING AT THE OPENING OF THE ROAD MADE BY THE SAMÓANS FOR MR. STEVENSON, OCTOBER 1894

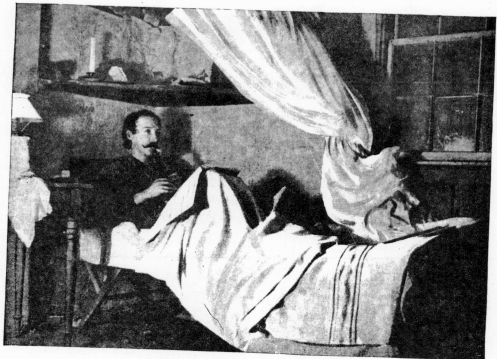

STEVENSON PLAYING HIS FLAGEOLET

sophical value lies in the fact that he realised this great paradox
that life becomes more fascinating the darker it grows, that life is
worth living only so far as it is difficult to live. The more stedfastly
and gloomily men clung to their sinister visions of duty, the more,
in his eyes, they swelled the chorus of the praise of things. He
was an optimist because to him everything was heroic, and nothing
more heroic than the pessimist. To Stevenson, the optimist,
belong the most frightful epigrams of pessimism. It was he
who said that this planet on which we live was more drenched with
blood, animal and vegetable, than a pirate ship. It was he who
said that man was a disease of the agglutinated dust. And his
supreme position and his supreme difference from all common

optimists is merely this, that all common optimists say that life is glorious in spite of these things, but he said that all life was glorious because of them. He discovered that a battle is more comforting than a truce. He discovered the same great fact which was discovered by a man so fantastically different from him that the mere name of him may raise a legitimate laugh —General Booth.

A PORTRAIT OF MRS. STRONG, STEVENSON'S STEP-DAUGHTER AND VALUED AMANUENSIS

He discovered, that is to say, that religious evolution might tend at last to the discovery, that the peace given in the churches was less attractive to the religious spirit than the war promised outside; that for one man who wanted to be comforted a hundred wanted to be stirred; that men, even ordinary men, wanted in the last resort, not life or death, but drums.

It may reasonably be said that of all outrageous comparisons one of the most curious must be this between the old evangelical despot and enthusiast and the elegant and almost hedonistic man of letters. But these far-fetched comparisons are infinitely the sanest, for they remind us of the sanest of all conceptions, the unity of things. A splendid and pathetic prince of India, living in far-off æons, came to many of the same conceptions as a rather dingy German professor in the nineteenth century; for there are many essential resemblances between Buddha and

THE SAN FRANCISCO
MEMORIAL TO
ROBERT LOUIS STEVENSON
Erected by public subscription
in 1897

Schopenhauer. And if any one should urge that lapse of time might produce mere imitation, it is easy to point out that the same great

Graham Balfour   Mrs. Osbourne

Hon. B. R. Wise

Robert Louis Stevenson   Mrs. Thomas Stevenson

From a photo kindly supplied by Mr. Graham Balfour

ROBERT LOUIS STEVENSON AT THE HOUSE OF THE HON. B. R. WISE, SYDNEY

theory of evolution was pronounced simultaneously by Darwin, who became so grim a rationalist that he ceased even to care for the

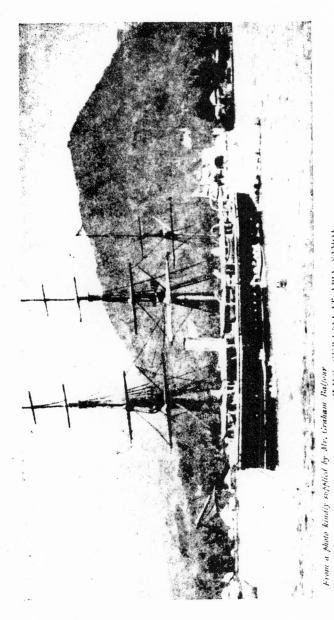

From a photo kindly supplied by Mrs. Graham Balfour

H.M.S. *CURAÇOA* AT APIA, SAMOA

The *Curaçoa*, with H.M.S. *Falke* and H.M.S. *Bussard*, took part in the bombardment of the rebels of Atua

arts, and by Wallace, who has become so fiery a spiritualist that he yearns after astrology and table-rapping. Men of the most widely divergent types are connected by these invisible cords across the world, and Stevenson was essentially a Colonel in the Salvation Army. He believed, that is to say, in making religion a military affair. His militarism, of course, needs to be carefully understood. It was considered entirely from the point of view of the person fighting. It had none of that evil pleasure in contemplating the killed and wounded,

From a photo by J. Davis, Apia, Samoa

ENTERTAINMENT GIVEN TO THE BAND OF THE *KATOOMBA* BY MR. AND MRS. ROBERT LOUIS STEVENSON AT VAILIMA

in realising the agonies of the vanquished, which has been turned by
some modern writers into an art, a literary sin, which, though only
painted in black ink on white paper, is far worse than the mere sin
of murder.   Stevenson's militarism was as free from all the mere

ROBERT LOUIS STEVENSON, FROM THE MEDALLION BY
A. ST. GAUDENS

poetry of conquest and dominion as the militarism of an actual
common soldier.   It was mainly, that is to say, a poetry of watches
and parades and camp-fires.   He knew he was in the hosts of the
Lord : he did not trouble much about the enemy.   Here is his
resemblance to that Church Militant, which, secure only in its own

rectitude, wages war upon the nameless thing which has tormented and bewildered us from the beginning of the world.

Of course, this Stevensonian view of war suggests in itself that other question, touching which so much has been written about him, the subject of childishness and the child. It is true, of course, that the splendidly infantile character of Stevenson's mind saved him from any evil arising from his militarism. A child can hit his nurse hard with a wooden sword without being an æsthete of violence. He may enjoy a hard whack, but he need not enjoy the colour harmonies of black and blue as they are presented in a bruise. It is undoubtedly the truth, of course, that Stevenson's interest in this fighting side of human nature was mainly childish, that is to say, mainly subjective. He thought of the whole matter in the primary colours of poetic simplicity. He said with splendid gusto in one of his finest letters:

THE TOMB OF
ROBERT LOUIS
STEVENSON
IN SAMOA

Reproduced from
" Islands of the
Southern Seas,"
by M. M. Shoemaker
by kind
permission of
Messrs. Putnam

LOTO ALOFA—
THE
"ROAD OF
THE
LOVING
HEART"

Cut by the
rebel chiefs
in order to
commemorate
Robert Louis
Stevenson's
kindness to them
during their
imprisonment
by the
European
Powers

Reproduced from
*Scribner's
Magazine*
by kind
permission
of the
publishers

" Shall we never taste blood ? " But he did not really want blood.
He wanted crimson-lake.

But of course, in the case of so light and elusive a figure as
Stevenson, even the terms which have been most definitely attached
to him tend to become misleading and inadequate, and the terms
" childlike " or " childish," true as they are down to a very fundamental
truth, are yet the origin of a certain confusion. One of the greatest
errors in existing literary philosphy is that of confusing the child with

the boy. Many great moral teachers, beginning with Jesus Christ, have perceived the profound philosophical importance of the child. The child sees everything freshly and fully ; as we advance in life it is true that we see things in some degree less and less, that we are afflicted, spiritually and morally, with the myopia of the student. But the problem of the boy is essentially different from that of the child. The boy represents the earliest growth of the earthly, unmanageable qualities, poetic still, but not so simple or so universal. The child enjoys the plain picture of the world : the boy wants the secret, the end of the story. The child wishes to dance in the sun ; but the boy wishes to sail after buried treasure. The child enjoys a flower, and the boy a mechanical engine. And the finest and most peculiar work of Stevenson is rather that he was the first writer to treat seriously and poetically the æsthetic instincts of the boy. He celebrated the toy gun rather than the rattle. Around the child and his rattle there has gathered a splendid service of literature and art ; Hans Andersen and Charles Kingsley and George Macdonald and Walter Crane and Kate Greenaway and a list of celebrities a mile long bring their splendid gifts to the christening. But the tragedy of the helpless infant (if it be a male infant—girls are quite a different matter) is simply this, that, having been fed on literature and art, as fine in its way as Shelley and Turner up to the age of seven, he feels within him new impulses and interests growing, a hunger for action and knowledge, for fighting and discovery, for the witchery of facts and the wild poetry of geography. And then he is suddenly dropped with a crash out of literature, and can read nothing but " Jack Valiant among the Indians." For in the whole scene there is only one book which is at once literature, like Hans Andersen, and yet a book for boys and not for children, and its name is " Treasure Island."

G. K. CHESTERTON.

THE LAST RESTING-PLACE OF ROBERT LOUIS STEVENSON ON THE SUMMIT OF MOUNT VAEA.

HOME FROM THE HILL.*

By W. ROBERTSON NICOLL.

"Home is the sailor, home from the sea,
And the hunter home from the hill." R. L. S.

LET the weary body lie
　Where he chose its grave,
'Neath the wide and starry sky,
　By the Southern wave:
While the island holds her trust
And the hill keeps faith,
Through the watches that divide
　The long night of death.

But the spirit, free from thrall,
　Now goes forth of these
To its birthright, and inherits
　Other lands and seas:
We shall find him when we seek him
　In an older home,—
By the hills and streams of childhood
　'Tis his weird to roam.

In the fields and woods we hear him
　Laugh and sing and sigh:
Or where by the Northern breakers
　Sea-birds troop and cry;
Or where over lonely moorlands
　Winter winds fly fleet;
Or by sunny graves he hearkens
　Voices low and sweet.

We have lost him, we have found him:
　Mother, he was fain
Nimbly to retrace his footsteps;
　Take his life again
To the breast that first had warmed it,
　To the tried and true,—
He has come, our well beloved,
　Scotland, back to you!

* First published in *Blackwood's Magazine*, February, 1895. Reprinted by kind permission of Messrs. Blackwood.

BIOGRAPHICAL NOTE

ROBERT LOUIS STEVENSON

" Thin-legged, thin-chested, slight unspeakably,
Neat-footed and weak-fingered : in his face—
Lean, large-boned, curved of beak, and touched with race,
Bold-lipped, rich-tinted, mutable as the sea,
The brown eyes radiant with vivacity—
There shines a brilliant and romantic grace,
A spirit intense and rare, with trace on trace
Of passion and impudence and energy."—W. E. HENLEY.

The birthplace of Robert Louis Stevenson
see page 3

Robert Louis Stevenson, only son of Thomas Stevenson, Civil Engineer, was born on November 13th, 1850, at No. 8, Howard Place, Edinburgh. The house was one of a row of unpretentious stone buildings, situated just north of the water of Leith. When Louis reached the age of two-and-a-half, a removal was made to a more commodious dwelling in Inverleith Terrace ; but this proving unsuitable to the child's delicate health, the family settled at No. 17, Heriot Row, which continued to be their Edinburgh home for thirty years.

No. 17, Heriot Row, Edinburgh
see page 5
Swanston Cottage
see page 7

Two other houses were closely connected with the pleasant memories of Stevenson's youth,—Swanston Cottage, the country residence of his parents, and Colinton Manse, the abode of his maternal grandfather. The situation and history of the former he described in " Picturesque Notes on Edinburgh," indeed, the cottage and its garden have been immortalised by Stevenson, both in prose and in verse. " Upon the main slope of the Pentlands . . . a bouquet of old trees stands round a white farmhouse, and from a neighbouring dell you can see smoke rising and leaves rustling in the breeze. Straight above, the hills climb a thousand feet into the air. The neighbourhood, about the time of lambs, is clamorous with the bleating of flocks ; and you will be awakened in the grey of early summer mornings by the barking of a dog, or the voice of a shepherd shouting to the echoes. This, with the hamlet lying behind unseen, is Swanston." But it was at Colinton that Stevenson passed the happiest days of his childhood. " Out of my reminiscences of life in that dear place, all the morbid and painful elements have disappeared," he wrote ; " I can recall nothing but sunshiny weather. That was my golden age : *et ego in Arcadia vixi.*" In " Memories and Portraits " he drew a vivid picture of the Manse. " It was a place at that time like no other ; the garden cut into provinces by a great hedge of beech, and overlooked by the church and the terrace of the churchyard, where the tombstones were thick, and after nightfall 'spunkies' might be seen to dance, at least by children ; flowerpots lying warm in sunshine ; laurels and the great yew making elsewhere a pleasing horror of shade ; the smell of water rising from all round, with an added tang of paper-mills ; the sound of water everywhere, and the sound of mills—the wheel and the dam singing their alternate strain ; the birds from every bush and from every corner of the overhanging woods pealing out their notes till the air throbbed with them ; and in the midst of all this the Manse."

Colinton Manse
see page 6

The Rev. Lewis Balfour, grandfather of Robert Louis Stevenson
see page 2

It was in the same essay that Stevenson described his grandfather, the Rev. Lewis Balfour, Minister of Colinton, as " of singular simplicity of nature ; unemotional, and hating the display of what he felt ; standing contented on the old ways ; a lover of his life and innocent habits to the end." " Now I often wonder," he added later, " what I have inherited from this old minister. I must suppose, indeed, that he was fond of preaching sermons, and so am I, though I never heard it maintained that either of us loved to hear them." Of his father, Stevenson wrote also in "Memories and Portraits." "He was a man of a somewhat antique strain; with a blended sternness and softness that was wholly Scottish, and at first somewhat bewildering; with a profound essential melancholy of disposition, and (what often accompanies it) the most humorous geniality in company; shrewd and childish; passionately attached, passionately prejudiced; a man of many extremes, many faults of temper, and no very stable foothold for himself among life's troubles." On the other hand, there is no descriptive sketch of

Stevenson's mother from his pen—a want probably accounted for by the fact that she survived him. In person she was tall and graceful; her vivacity and brightness were most attractive, and some idea of her undaunted energy and spirit may be gathered from Mr. Cope Cornford's "Robert Louis Stevenson," in which he says of Mrs. Thomas Stevenson, "At past sixty, after a lifetime of conventional Edinburgh, this lady broke up the house in Heriot Row, removed herself and her belongings to Apia, learned to ride bare-backed and to go bare-footed, and took on the life at Vailima and the life of Tusitala's native friends with equal gusto and intelligence. Stevenson was fond of calling himself a tramp and a gipsy, and that he could do so with justice was owing to the fact that his mother was Margaret Balfour."

Another important factor in his early life was the devotion of his nurse, Alison Cunningham, "Cummy," as he invariably called her, whose care during his ailing childhood did so much both to preserve his life and foster his love of tales and poetry, and of whom, until his death, he thought with the utmost constancy of affection. "My dear old nurse," he wrote to her, "—and you know there is nothing a man can say nearer his heart, except his mother or his wife—my dear old nurse, God will make good to you all the good that you have done, and mercifully forgive you all the evil."

In his nurse's possession there remains a treasured album containing a series of photographs of Robert Louis Stevenson, dating from babyhood

onwards: the first, as an infant on his mother's knee; the second, at the age of twenty months; and again, at four years old, with bright, dark eyes, wide apart, and stiff curls framing his face. In the next, taken at the age of six, his hair is cropped to a manlike shortness. His hands have lost their baby podginess, and are nervous, long-fingered. He has a whip in his grasp, which falls slackly down, as if toys were not in his line, and he looks pensively ahead. A few years later he was photographed with his father, on whose shoulder one hand is resting, the other being tucked, boyishly, into his pocket. "Stevenson calls himself 'ugly' in his student days," writes Mr. Baildon; "but I think this is a term that never at any time fitted him. Certainly to him as a boy about fourteen (with the creed which he propounded to me, that at sixteen one was a man) it would not apply. In body Stevenson was assuredly badly set up. His limbs were long and lean and spidery, and his chest flat, so as almost to suggest some malnutrition, such sharp angles and corners did his joints make under his clothes. But in his face this was belied. His brow was oval and full, over soft brown eyes,

that seemed already to have drunk the sunlight under southern vines. The whole face had a tendency to an oval Madonna-like type. But about the mouth and in the mirthful, mocking light of the eyes, there lingered ever a ready Autolycus roguery, that rather suggested the sly god Hermes masquerading as a mortal. The eyes were always genial, however gaily the lights danced in them; but about the mouth there was something a little tricksy and mocking, as of a spirit that already peeped behind the scenes of life's pageant and more than guessed its unrealities."

Three-and-a-half years were employed by Stevenson in preparation for the profession of civil engineer. He spent the winter and sometimes the summer sessions at the University of Edinburgh. In 1871, however, he informed his father of his inclination to follow literary pursuits. Engineering was given up forthwith, and it was arranged that he should study for the Scottish Bar, to which he was called in July 1875.

In the photograph on page 13 you have him "bewigged as Robert Louis Stevenson, Advocate, and there is the suspicion of a playful duplicity in the would-be wisdom-framed face."

It was at this period that Stevenson came in close companionship with Sir Walter Simpson, "the Bart.," who was also studying Law. Sir Walter figured as "The Cigarette" to Stevenson's "Arethusa" in "The Inland Voyage."

From the days of his toy theatre onwards, Robert Louis Stevenson had always taken an intense interest in matters theatrical, and, with another of his friends, Fleeming Jenkin, he took part in numerous amateur performances. The portrait in fancy dress was no doubt the outcome of this favourite pursuit.

On his return with Sir Walter Simpson from the Inland Voyage, Stevenson became acquainted with Mrs. Osbourne, who was later to become his wife. The marriage took place in San Francisco in the spring of 1880.

In the hope of finding a climate suited to his health, Stevenson went abroad at the close of 1882, and settled for a time at Hyères, where, by the end of March 1883, he was established in a house of his own—the Chalet La Solitude. This was a picturesque cottage, built in the Swiss manner, on the slope of the hill just above the town, and here, for some eight or nine months, he enjoyed the happiest period of his life. "We all dwell together and make fortunes in the loveliest house you ever saw, with a garden like a fairy story, and a view like a classical landscape," he wrote. "Little? Well, it is not large. But it is Eden and Beulah and the Delectable Mountains and Eldorado and the Hesperidean Isles and Bimini."

Year after year the struggle against ill-health was increasing, and in 1887 Stevenson's uncle, Dr. George Balfour, insisted on a complete change of climate, and a second voyage to America was undertaken. In the following June began the South Sea cruises, which, after three years of wandering, culminated in the period of settled residence at Samoa.

While in the South Seas, in 1889, Stevenson paid a visit to Molokai, the leper settlement in the Hawaiian Islands, which resulted in his famous "Letter to Dr. Hyde," in defence of Father Damian, who died a month previous to his arrival. "The place as regards scenery is grand, gloomy, and bleak," he wrote, describing the settlement. "Mighty mountain walls descending sheer along the whole face of the island into a sea unusually deep; the front of the mountain, ivied and furred with clinging forest, one viridescent cliff; about half way, from east to west, the low, bare, stony promontory edged in between the cliff and the ocean; the two little towns (Kalawao and Kalaupapa) seated on either side of it, as bare almost as bathing machines upon a beach; and the population gorgons and chimæras dire."

About three miles inland, on the hills above Apia (the chief town of Upolu in the Samoan group), the Stevensons made their home in November 1890. The house itself was erected on a clearing of some three hundred acres, between two streams, from the westernmost of which the steep side of Vaea mountain, covered with forest, rose to a height of thirteen hundred feet above the sea. From this stream and its four tributaries the estate was called Vailima, the Samoan name for Five Waters. "This is a hard and interesting and beautiful life that we lead now," he wrote. "Our place is in a deep cleft of Vaea mountain, some six hundred feet above the sea, embowered in forest, which is our strangling enemy and which we combat with axes and dollars." The house was built of wood throughout, painted a dark green outside, with a red roof of corrugated iron. The building was finally enlarged in compatibility with the requirements of the family, and consisted, after December 1892, of three rooms, bath, storeroom, and cellars below, with five bedrooms and library upstairs. On the ground floor a verandah, twelve feet deep, ran in front of the whole house and along one side of it. The chief feature of the interior was the large hall. "My house is a great place," he added on another occasion; "we have a hall fifty feet long, with a great red-wood stair ascending from it, where we dine in state." The two posts of the big staircase were guarded by a couple of Burmese gilded idols.

Dining- and reception-hall at Vailima
see page 21

Stevenson gave many glimpses of his life at Vailima in his letters to Mr. Sidney Colvin. The following extract seems typical :—" I know pleasure still ; pleasure with a thousand faces and none perfect, a thousand tongues all broken, a thousand hands and all of them with scratching nails. High among these I place the delight of weeding out here alone by the garrulous water, under the silence of the high wood, broken by incongruous sounds of birds. And take my life all through, look at it fore and back and upside down—though I would very fain change myself—I would not change my circumstances."

Stevenson and his favourite horse, "Jack"
see page 23

His favourite exercise was riding, and he was an excellent horseman. "Jack," the New Zealand pony which he bought in 1890, carried him well. "I do not say my Jack is anything extraordinary, he is only an island horse, and the profane might call him a Punch, and his face is like a donkey's, and natives have ridden him and he has no mouth in consequence, and occasionally shies. But his merits are equally surprising, and I don't think I should ever have known Jack's merits if I had not been riding up of late on moonless nights."

Entertainment given to the band of the *Katoomba* by the Stevensons
see page 30

It was Stevenson's great delight to keep open house at Vailima, and especially to organise any festivity in which the natives could share. An example of this hospitality was the entertainment given to the band of the *Katoomba*, on September 12th, 1893. " I got leave from Captain Bickford to have the band of the *Katoomba* come up, and they came, fourteen of 'em, with drum, fife, cymbals and bugles, blue jackets, white caps, and smiling faces. The house was all decorated with scented greenery above and below. We had not only our nine outdoor workers, but a contract party that we took on in charity to pay their war-fine; the band besides, as it came up the mountain, had collected a following of children by the way, and we had a picking of Samoan ladies to receive them. They played to us, they danced, they sang, they tumbled."

Tembinoka, the King of Apemama
see page 24

Stevenson's influence with the natives was probably as great as that of any white resident in the islands. He was certainly respected by them as a whole, and by many he was beloved. Indeed, his friendship with Tembinoka, the king of Apemama, whose character is described in "The South Seas," forms an important episode in that volume. "He is the Napoleon of the group, poet, tyrant, altogether a man of mark. 'I got power,' is his favourite word ; it interlards his conversation." Another chief, with whom Stevenson was in great sympathy, was Mataafa, the "rebel" king who was defeated and banished in August 1893, upon outbreak of war in the island. Mataafa he believed to be the one man of governing capacity among the native chiefs, and it was his desire that the Powers should conciliate rather than crush him. "Mataafa is the nearest thing to a hero in my history, and really a fine fellow ; plenty of sense, and the most dignified, quiet, gentle manners.'

Mataafa, the "Rebel" King
see page 24

During Stevenson's four years' residence in Samoa, no fewer than eight British men-of-war entered the harbour, and at the time of the bombardment of the rebels of Atua, H.M.S. *Curaçoa* was more often stationed at Apia than any of the others. "We have in port the model warship of Great Britain," he wrote, describing a cruise to Manùa; "she is called the *Curaçoa* . . . a ship that I would guarantee to go anywhere it was possible for men to go, and accomplish anything it was permitted man to attempt."

After taking up his abode at Vailima, Stevenson only twice returned to the world of populous cities. In the early part of 1893 he spent several weeks in Sydney, where he visited his friend, the Hon. B. R. Wise. In September of the same year he made a voyage to Honolulu. On his return to Apia in November, he was gratified by the mark of esteem and gratitude extended to him by the native chiefs, who cleared, dug, and completed the road to Vailima—till then a mere track, which could only be traversed in dry weather by wagons or by a buggy, goods being taken to the house by two New Zealand pack-horses. On the estate itself the route lay by a lane of limes, and this was cut off by the Ala Loto Alofa, or "Road of the Loving Heart," which the chiefs cut to commemorate Stevenson's kindness to them during their imprisonment by the European Powers. "Considering the great love of Tusitala, in his loving care of us in our distress in the prison, we have therefore prepared a splendid gift. It shall never be muddy, it shall endure for ever, this road that we have dug." Upon its completion a great Kava drinking was held, there was a solemn returning of thanks, and Stevenson gave an address, which was his best and most outspoken utterance to the people of Samoa.

Only two months later, on December 3rd, 1894, Stevenson died. He was in his forty-fifth year. The Union Jack which flew over the house was hauled down and placed over the body as it lay in the hall where he had spent some of the most delightful hours of his life.

"His devoted Samoans cut an almost perpendicular pathway to the top of the mountain Vaea, which he had designed as his last resting-place. Thither with almost herculean labours they bore him, and decked his grave with costly presents, of the most valuable and highly-prized mats. There he lies, by a strange, almost ironic fate, under other stars than ours. Driven forth, not, thank God, by neglect nor by any injustice of man, but by the scourge of sickness and threat of death and the unfriendliness of his native skies, into his beautiful exile amid tropic seas, he draws, and long will draw, perhaps while the language lasts, with a strange tenderness, the hearts of men to that far and lonely Samoan mount."

On the tombstone, built of great blocks of cement, are carved the Scotch thistle and the native ante, and between them is a bronze plate bearing the following inscription, his own requiem :—

> " Under the wide and starry sky
> Dig the grave and let me die ;
> Glad did I live and gladly die,
> And I laid me down with a will.
> This be the verse you grave for me,—
> Here he lies where he longed to be ;
> Home is the sailor, home from the sea,
> And the hunter home from the hill."

Printed by Hazell, Watson & Viney, Ld., London and Aylesbury.